Tune-In

Heaven

Blessings, Protection and Joy

Abridged Edition

Leonard Zagurskie, Jr.

~

Tune-In Heaven,
Blessings, Protection & Joy
Abridged Edition

By Leonard Zagurskie, Jr.

Published by Leonard Zagurskie, Jr.

Cover Design and Drawings
by Leonard Zagurskie, Jr.

Editing Assist
by Regina Aflleje Zagurskie

Contents

Tune-In Heaven
Introduction

There is a Higher Power. There are fixed precepts that
shape our lives in this world and in the next. If you know
them then you can make choices so that you receive the
blessings, the Lord's Joy, Protection and Prosperity or
otherwise your life appears fortuitous and you repeat
cycles and behaviors. Are you interested in making
positive changes in life and receiving the Blessings and
the Protection of God Almighty, and entering into the Joy
of the Lord, the Higher Power, the Creator God, the
Protector, the Holy One, the Redeemer? Then to Tune-In
Heaven, you need to know these seven precepts so you
can be aware when these choices are presented:

➢ Truth. You cannot benefit from false doctrine. You
   can only benefit from knowing the truth and acting
   upon the truth. For example, if you have a phony bus
   schedule then sometimes you catch a bus and other
   times a bus never comes. Just like catching a bus your
   life appears fortuitous. Truth is worthy even so much
   more worthy than a true bus schedule. Truth is wholly
   worthy.

- ➢ The Higher Power, Creator God of the Universe, the Good Heavenly Father, the Redeemer, gave you the power to choose.

- ➢ If you complain then there is where you get stuck. Delight and commit one's way to the Lord. Obey His Commandments. Tune-In Blessings, Prosperity and Joy!

- ➢ What you hold in your heart then that is what you attract. The God of the Universe, the Higher Power, the Good Heavenly Father that loves you and desires to give you the good desires of your heart is wholly worthy. And, you will get the desires of your heart!

- ➢ The only behavior you can change is your own behavior. Trying to change someone else's behavior is manipulation also it is witchcraft.

TUNE-IN HEAVEN INTRODUCTION

➤ When evil is intended, the Higher Power, the God of the universe, the Good Heavenly Father, the Holy One, the Redeemer, Who knows and loves His own and they know Him, the Protector thwarts the evil and brings about justice and makes it for good to be achieved.

Vengeance is the Lords. When evil is intended against you He redirects it back to sender and utterly destroys the evil or the Lord means it for good, many are saved and He lets you enter into His Joy and gives you the good desires of your heart and is wholly worthy.

➤ You can have a personal relationship with the Higher Power, the Holy One, the God of the Universe, the Good Heavenly Father, the Creator God, the Redeemer.

The Lord is accessible from any place at any time. He is now reaching out to you as the prophet Isaiah declares: "God's arms are stretched out still." You can picture Jesus on the cross with His outstretched arms, and now His arms are stretched out to us to enter into His Joy and receive His Blessings, Prosperity and Protection.

And now imagine knowing these precepts that shape our lives in this world and in the next, accordingly you can choose the Lord's Blessings, Joy, Protection and Prosperity.

As many of you already know there absolutely is a Higher Power, the Holy One, the Holy Spirit, who is the Creator of the Universe, the Redeemer. He wants to give you the good desires of your heart. He is the Good Heavenly Father.

You are Tuning Into Heaven as you learn these Biblical precepts. Also you will more easily recognize the Lord in the Scriptures the closer you get to know the Lord. He reveals himself more to you as the more you get to know His precepts.

And the closer you get to the Lord the more Blessings you will receive right here, right now, today and the Joy of the Lord that surpasses all understanding.

Just as one recognizes someone who will become a friend and then becomes a friend so it is with the Higher Spirit, the Holy One, the Redeemer, the Creator God of the Universe who is the Good Heavenly Father. When you read any one of the four Gospels of the New Testament you begin to recognize the Lord by His Words.

Jesus is the good shepherd. He knows His sheep and they know Him. The Gospel of John:

▶ 14. I am the good shepherd, and know my sheep, and am known of mine.

15. As the Father knoweth me, even so know I the Father: and I lay down my life for the sheep.

John 10: 14-1

The Bible illustrates real individuals, not storybook characters, yes, real individuals with actual personal relationships with the Higher Power, the God of the Universe, the Holy One, the Redeemer who experienced the Protection, the Blessings and Joy of the Lord. The details of their struggles and heartfelt emotions are experienced as you read and learn these precepts when you read the Bible. Read the Bible the awesome word of the Lord.

The focus of "Tuning in Heaven" is on identifying and outlining these precepts. With knowing, choosing and applying these precepts you too can enter into the Blessings, the Prosperity, the Joy and the Protection of the Higher Power, the Higher Spirit, the Holy One, the Lord, the Creator God, God Almighty, the Good Heavenly Father, the Redeemer.

Tune-In Heaven, the Abridged Edition introduces these precepts to the reader to thoroughly become aware and grow conscious of these life-changing precepts read the full-length Tune-In Heaven, First Edition.

TUNE-IN HEAVEN INTRODUCTION

When you are informed for the very first time with any precept in this book it is truly an amazing, real eye opener - a life changer, because these principles are absolutely real and utterly life transforming. As you will learn!

You too can learn these precepts, apply them and Tune-In Heaven.

As you Tune-In Heaven and become more aware of the Higher Spirit, the Creator God of the Universe, the Holy One, the Lord, the Redeemer you experience the Blessings and the Protection of the Lord and enter into the Joy, of God Almighty.

To thoroughly become aware and grow conscious of these life-changing precepts read the full-length Tune-In Heaven, First Edition.

- - - - - - -

WHAT YOU NEED TO KNOW ABOUT BIBLICAL QUOTED SCRIPTURES AND REFERENCES IN THIS BOOK:

All Biblical quoted scriptures and references in this book are from the King James Version (KJV) of the Bible.

KJV scriptures are presented in the KJV format with no changes to the outdated wording and spelling.

The symbol: ▶ indicates that scripture from the KJV of the Bible follows.

Immediately before quoted scripture "Notes" provide helpful definitions of words used in the upcoming scripture.

After the quoted KJV scripture then on the next line is stated the Bible book, chapter and verse.

CHAPTER 1

~

No Complaining

The first precept you must learn is to stop complaining!
No matter what picture you have in your mind of Heaven,
it does not include complaining. Can you imagine Apostle

Paul, Apostle Peter or anyone complaining about
anything in Heaven, for example, that the golden streets
are somewhat less than spectacular? Of course not! You
cannot "Tune Into" the Blessings of the Lord if you
complain - then there is where you get stuck. Read on to
learn how this precept works.

In the old days they used the word "murmuring" which
means complaining.

When reading Bible verses about complaining substitute complaining for murmuring:

Note: the destroyer is Satan.

▶ Neither murmur ye, as some of them also murmured, and were destroyed of the destroyer.

1 Corinthians 10:10

▶ Do all things without murmurings and disputings,

Philippians 2:14

▶ In every thing give thanks: for this is the will of God in Christ Jesus concerning you.

1 Thessalonians 5:18

▶ Let no corrupt communication proceed out of your mouth, but that, which is good to the use of edifying, that it may minister grace unto the hearers.

Ephesians 4:29

▶ Not that I speak in respect of want: for I have learned, in whatsoever state I am, therewith to be content.

Philippians 4:11

CHAPTER 1
NO COMPLAINING

▶ A merry heart doeth good like a medicine: but a broken spirit drieth the bones.

Proverbs 17:22

OK you may say, I got it: The Bible says not to complain. But how does this relate to "Tuning into Heaven" and receiving the Blessings of the Higher Power?

Answer: First, the Blessings come from the Lord, God Almighty, the Protector, the Higher Power the Creator God, the Good Heavenly Father, the Holy One, the Redeemer. He is the source of the Blessings:

▶ But thou shalt remember the LORD thy God: for it is he that giveth thee power to get wealth, that he may establish his covenant which he sware unto thy fathers, as it is this day.

Deuteronomy 8:18

▶ Thus saith the LORD, thy Redeemer, the Holy One of Israel; I am the LORD thy God which teacheth thee to profit, which leadeth thee by the way that thou shouldest go.

Isaiah 48:17

▶ The blessing of the LORD, it maketh rich, and he addeth no sorrow with it.

Proverbs 10:22

How to Love the Lord:

So if the Blessings come from the Higher Power, God Almighty, the Creator God, the Good Heavenly Father, the Holy One, the Redeemer, then how does one "Tune Into" these Blessings?

Answer: You must love the Lord, which means to follow His Commandments:

▶ If you love me, keep my commands.
John 14:15

▶ That I may cause those that love me to inherit substance; and I will fill their treasures.

Proverbs 8:21

▶Jesus answered and said unto him, If a man love me, he will keep my words: and my Father will love him, and we will come unto him, and make our abode with him.

John 14: 23

CHAPTER 1
NO COMPLAINING

How to Love One Another:

Loving the Lord is keeping His Commandments therefore
love requires action. Love is what one does. Love is
behavior. Love is how one treats another. Love is much
more than just saying sweet nothings, empty words and
excess dramatics. Love is action: Treating another one
with respect, kindly and considerate of feelings - that is
love. Love is expressed and measured by how one has
treated another and what one has done for another. It is
not just saying it: It is doing it!

You do for someone things that they like and desire. Not
what you like and enjoy. You need to be observant as to
what they enjoy. Then that is what you do.

Note: Take caution. Being taken advantage of is not love.
It is being beguiled, swindled and cheated.

Loving the Lord and Receiving His Blessings:

So then "loving the Lord," which is keeping His commandments ensures us of His blessings.

Deuteronomy 28: 1-14 fully explains and describes the Lord's Blessings:

The Lord's Blessings:

► 1. And it shall come to pass, if thou shalt hearken diligently unto the voice of the LORD thy God, to observe and to do all his commandments which I command thee this day, that the LORD thy God will set thee on high above all nations of the earth:

2. And all these blessings shall come on thee, and overtake thee, if thou shalt hearken unto the voice of the LORD thy God.

3. Blessed shalt thou be in the city, and blessed shalt thou be in the field.

4. Blessed shall be the fruit of thy body, and the fruit of thy ground, and the fruit of thy cattle, the increase of thy kine, and the flocks of thy sheep.

5. Blessed shall be thy basket and thy store.

6. Blessed shalt thou be when thou comest in, and blesse shalt thou be when thou goest out.

CHAPTER 1
NO COMPLAINING

7. The LORD shall cause thine enemies that rise up against thee to be smitten before thy face: they shall come out against thee one way, and flee before thee seven ways.

8. The LORD shall command the blessing upon thee in thy storehouses, and in all that thou settest thine hand unto; and he shall bless thee in the land which the LORD thy God giveth thee.

9. The LORD shall establish thee an holy people unto himself, as he hath sworn unto thee, if thou shalt keep the commandments of the LORD thy God, and walk in his ways.

10. And all people of the earth shall see that thou art called by the name of the LORD; and they shall be afraid of thee.

11. And the LORD shall make thee plenteous in goods, in the fruit of thy body, and in the fruit of thy cattle, and in the fruit of thy ground, in the land which the LORD sware unto thy fathers to give thee.

12. The LORD shall open unto thee his good treasure, the heaven to give the rain unto thy land in his season, and to bless all the work of thine hand: and thou shalt lend unto many nations, and thou shalt not borrow.

13. And the LORD shall make thee the head, and not the tail; and thou shalt be above only, and thou shalt not be beneath; if that thou hearken unto the commandments of the LORD thy God, which I command thee this day, to observe and to do them:

14. And thou shalt not go aside from any of the words, which I command thee this day, to the right hand, or to the left, to go after other gods to serve them.

Deuteronomy 28: 1-14

So what is the point?

Answer: **You get blessings when you follow the Lord's Commandments.**

The Lord's Ten Commandments are found in the Bible in Exodus 20:2-17 and in Deuteronomy 5:6-21. Other commandments such as "no complaining" are not as well recognized. But profoundly impact the Blessings, the Protection and the Joy.

CHAPTER 1
NO COMPLAINING

Why would complaining profoundly impact Blessings?

Answer: Complaining is not obeying the Lord. Not obeying the Lord is sinning.

In the Bible, in Deuteronomy 28: 15-45, the curses of disobedience are listed. Clearly the curses are the direct opposite of the blessings. Complaining not only blocks the Blessings but also attracts the Lord's curses!

So then if one complains then there is where one gets stuck. The cycle repeats. Complaining blocks the Blessings and attracts the Lord's curses!

Also the Lord is a fair and just Lord, so He will only hold you accountable for what you know. So you know now and you can no longer use that excuse. It is better that you know. This way you can Tune-In the Blessings, Prosperity and Joy.

As most of the readers know if you ask Jesus to forgive you for your sins He will forgive you for any sin.

The Jurisdiction of the Lord is the Heart.

He knows your heart.
Note: Countenance means face.

▶ But the Lord said unto Samuel, Look not on his countenance, or on the height of his stature; because I have refused him: for the Lord seeth not as man seeth; for man looketh on the outward appearance, but the Lord looketh on the heart.

1 Samuel 16:7

You can personally approach the Lord in prayer and ask to be forgiven and He will forgive you. You can do that right now and He will forgive you. If you desire to reconcile with the Lord, in prayer, call upon the name of the Lord and ask Him for forgiveness. Also, please keep in mind that many folks after asking the Lord for forgiveness then unfortunately the learning ends and the experience fades. Instead you can revitalize your faith, or make it the beginning: Keep learning and knowing God more. Delight and commit one's way to the Lord. Obey His Commandments. Tune-In Heaven.

Righteous Indignation Anger:

God's anger is an extensive fascinating topic. God is angered by sin. Likewise we are angered by sin. In the Bible are examples of the Lord's Holy Anger, referred to as the Lord's Righteous Indignation Anger. Sin such as complaining can kindle the Lord's anger. After the Lord delivered the Hebrews out of the bondage of slavery in Egypt the complaining of some of the Hebrews displeased the Lord and the Lord's fire consumed them:

▶ 1. And when the people complained, it displeased the Lord: and the Lord heard it; and his anger was kindled; and the fire of the Lord burnt among them, and consumed them that were in the uttermost parts of the camp.

2. And the people cried unto Moses; and when Moses prayed unto the Lord, the fire was quenched.

Numbers 11:1-2

The Lord is the champion of strangers (immigrants/aliens), widows and the fatherless children. The Lord warns not to harass, terrorize or cause problems for strangers, widows and the fatherless child, as He will hear their cry, His wrath will wax hot and the Lord will take the offender's life:

▶ 21. Thou shalt neither vex a stranger, nor oppress him: for ye were strangers in the land of Egypt.

22. Ye shall not afflict any widow, or fatherless child.

23. If thou afflict them in any wise, and they cry at all unto me, I will surely hear their cry;

24. And my wrath shall wax hot, and I will kill you with the sword; and your wives shall be widows, and your children fatherless.

Exodus 22: 21-24

As God is angered by sin in a very similar way so are we angered by sin. We are not to take matters into our own hands, except for very limited circumstances such as to save life: We are law and order!

We can tell it like it is and let the truth be known! Truth is wholly worthy. We are not complaining. We are voicing our concerns. We have no joy in sin! Vengeance is the Lords.

When evil is intended He thwarts the evil and brings about justice and makes good be achieved.

▶ Be ye angry, and sin not: let not the sun go down upon your wrath:

Ephesians 4:26

Fortunately for us, sinful mankind, the Lord is Abundant in Mercy, Grace and is Slow to Anger:

Note: chide means reprimand.

▶ 8. The Lord is merciful and gracious, slow to anger, and plenteous in mercy.

9. He will not always chide: neither will he keep his anger for ever

10. He hath not dealt with us after our sins; nor rewarded us according to our iniquities.

11. For as the heaven is high above the earth, so great is his mercy toward them that fear him.

12. As far as the east is from the west, so far hath he removed our transgressions from us.

13. Like as a father pitieth his children, so the Lord pitieth them that fear him.

14. For he knoweth our frame; he remembereth that we are dust.

15. As for man, his days are as grass: as a flower of the field, so he flourisheth.

16. For the wind passeth over it, and it is gone; and the place thereof shall know it no more.

17. But the mercy of the Lord is from everlasting to everlasting upon them that fear him, and his righteousness unto children's children;

Psalm 103:8-17

The Lord Loves You and Wants to Give You the Good Desires of your Heart:

The Higher Power, the Creator of the Universe, the Holy One, the Good Heavenly Father, the Redeemer wants to give you the good desires of your heart as Jesus explains:

▶ 7. Ask, and it shall be given you; seek, and ye shall find; knock, and it shall be opened unto you:

CHAPTER 1
NO COMPLAINING

8. For every one that asketh receiveth; and he that seeketh findeth; and to him that knocketh it shall be opened.

9. Or what man is there of you, whom if his son ask bread, will he give him a stone?

10. Or if he ask a fish, will he give him a serpent?

11. If ye then, being evil, know how to give good gifts unto your children, how much more shall your Father which is in heaven give good things to them that ask him?

Luke 11:7-11

The Lord loves you and wants to give you the good desires of your heart. But if you complain there is where you get stuck. Think of the parents who gives their child a gift and then the child complains about the gift. How does the parents feel?
So how do you think the Lord feels when one complains?

Stop Complaining!

Stop Complaining, Instead Give the Lord Thanks.

Stop complaining. Plainly you will be more content. Instead give thanks to the Lord as the Bible directs:

▶ In every thing give thanks: for this is the will of God in Christ Jesus concerning you.

1 Thessalonians 5:18

▶ And whatsoever ye do in word or deed, [do] all in the name of the Lord Jesus, giving thanks to God and the Father by him.

Colossians 3:17

▶ Fear thou not; for I [am] with thee: be not dismayed; for I [am] thy God: I will strengthen thee; yea, I will help thee; yea, I will uphold thee with the right hand of my righteousness.

Isaiah 41:10

Thank the Lord right now for getting to know the Higher Power the Creator God, the Good Heavenly Father, the Holy One, the Redeemer, so much better. He is now reaching out to you and now you know Him better.

CHAPTER 1
NO COMPLAINING

STOP COMPLAINING so that you receive the Blessings, the Lord's Joy, Protection and Prosperity or otherwise your life appears fortuitous and you repeat cycles and behaviors. Are you interested in making positive changes in life and receiving the Blessings, the Protection of God Almighty?

Tune Into the Lord's Blessings.

HERE ARE YOUR GIFTS

THANK YOU

I HATE IT!

Gift

Gift

Are you pleasing the Lord?

One can receive the Gifts of the Lord with thanks or one can cast away the Gifts of the Lord with complaints

Stop complaining and in everything give thanks!

If you are interested in entering into the Joy of the Lord, the Higher Power the Creator God, the Good Heavenly Father, the Holy One, the Redeemer stop complaining and in everything give thanks!

When one complains then there is where one gets stuck. Complaining blocks the Blessings and attracts the Lord's curses! The cycles repeat.

Become observant so that you can see in other people when they are complaining and how the patterns and cycles continue and how they are stuck there. Also you will see it in yourself. You will catch yourself complaining. So then the next time, catch yourself about to complain, then instead of complaining just thank the Lord. You have many countless reasons to thank the Lord.

If for example you are in a traffic jam, thank the Lord that you already stopped for gas before you ramped onto the expressway.

If you are running out of gas thank the Lord that you have a cell phone and can telephone roadside assistance, and so on and so on. Everyone knows that there is someone else out there going through a much worse encounter.

CHAPTER 1
NO COMPLAINING

And thank the Lord right now for getting to know the Higher Power the Creator God, the Good Heavenly Father, the Holy One, the Redeemer, a great deal better. He is now reaching out to you and now you know Him even better.

I use to complain because every time that I was driving my car and I would come to a highway exit - it was so incredible, it continually reoccurred - a big truck, driving in the traffic would every time be blocking my view of the exit sign of the exit that I needed to take. I would vehemently complain!

So after I understood not to complain but to give thanks, then I gave thanks to the Lord. Therefore, instead the next time that a big truck started blocking the exit, I started to thank the Lord that I had enough time to get over and properly exit and I thanked the Lord for many, many other things as well!

I thanked the Lord instead of complaining and the reoccurring circumstance of the big truck blocking the exit sign stopped!

Yes, it is true. You try it. See it for yourself! Become aware of what you are complaining about. Then exchange whatever you are complaining about with Thanks to the Lord.

Thank you Jesus!

Give the Lord thanks in all things! You will not only become more contented, you will free yourself from being stuck, you will please the Lord and obtain the Blessings and Protection of God Almighty, the Higher Power the Creator God, the Good Heavenly Father, the Holy One, the Redeemer.

Thank you Lord! Thank you Father, Son and Holy Spirit.

GOD GAVE US THE POWER TO CHOOSE

The Higher Power the Creator God, the Good Heavenly Father, the Holy One, the Redeemer, has given us the power to choose from the very beginning.

Ever since the Lord made the Garden of Eden for Adam and Eve, God Almighty desired our lives to be joy.
Adam and Eve were empowered with the ability to make a decision –
a choice. We have freedom of choice. Always choose joy and choose to do the right thing.

<u>Freedom of Choice</u>: **Always Choose Joy and Choose to Do the Right Thing!**

Guideline, Steps:

First, you always have one out of three (3) basic choices. Out of the three basic choices: Choose joy.

Next you are presented with two (2) conflicting, opposing and incompatible choices, the Lord or Satan, synonymously good or evil. Always choose the Lord and do the right thing.

Instructions, Explanations:

First: how do I choose Joy out of three (3) basic choices?

Answer: It is easy to make a positive decision to choose joy. The mind receives information (experiences), processes the information (thinking), then you make a decision (choice).

An example of making a positive decision to choose joy out of three (3) choices is presented in the following hypothetical event: A hypothetical person named Joe was just informed that his vehicle was demolished, totaled, completely destroyed, in the parking lot as a result of being slammed into by an out of control huge truck.

While Joe is processing this information let us suppose that Joe's vehicle was fully insured, although one hundred (100) percent financed, but historically unreliable and prior to the slam the vehicle's transmission had spun-out in the parking lot, so then earlier it was in need of a tow to the shop. Now can you see the smile start to appear on Joe's face!

Joe knows that the insurance will completely pay off the vehicle loan, the vehicle will be towed away and Joe will be able to get a replacement vehicle. Joe chooses to be happy.

CHAPTER 1
NO COMPLAINING

But wait a minute let us reverse the hypothetical facts. Let us say that the vehicle ran perfect, was historically dependable and that Joe absolutely needed the vehicle to go on a job interview the next morning at eight o'clock. Because Joe's unemployment compensation ended a week ago, he is out of money and he had received an eviction notice, so Joe absolutely needs to gets to that eight o'clock interview. Can you see that smile getting wiped off of Joe's face?

Joy: Joe has a third choice:

Joy is different than happy. Happy is derived from happenstance. Happenstance is an occurrence by chance: Choice based on happenstance leads to a roller coaster ride of emotions, whereas, Joy is a gift from the Lord. Joy is enduring, unchanging and steadfast. James the brother of Jesus instructs us to consider all trials and tribulations joy.

Note: divers means diverse/various.

Note: temptations also translates as trials.

▶ My brethren, count it all joy when ye fall into divers temptations;

James 1:2

Choosing joy, not complaining, praising and giving thanks to the Lord develops trust in the Lord. Trusting in the Lord gives way to entering into the Joy of the Lord. No better example of Joy and the enduring, steadfast Trust in the Lord than Psalm 30 by King David.

▶ 11. Thou hast turned for me my mourning into dancing: thou hast put off my sackcloth, and girded me with gladness;

12. To the end that my glory may sing praise to thee, and not be silent. O LORD my God, I will give thanks unto thee forever.
Psalm 30: 11-12

Praise you Lord, Praise you Jesus, Thank you Father, Son and Holy Spirit. I choose to thank and praise you Lord. I break out into praising the Lord. Praise the Lord as found in another Psalm by King David:

▶ 1. Praise ye the Lord. Praise God in his sanctuary: praise him in the firmament of his power.

2. Praise him for his mighty acts: praise him according to his excellent greatness.

3. Praise him with the sound of the trumpet: praise him with the psaltery and harp.

4. Praise him with the timbrel and dance: praise him with stringed instruments and organs.

5. Praise him upon the loud cymbals: praise him upon the high sounding cymbals.

6. Let every thing that hath breath praise the Lord. Praise ye the Lord.

Psalm 150: 1-6

CHAPTER 2

~

What you hold in your heart then that is what you attract

The Higher Power, the Creator God, the Good Heavenly Father, the Holy One, the Redeemer gave you the power to make choices. So then what shapes our decisions to make a specific choice is our beliefs, our desires and also outside influences. The beliefs you hold in your heart shape your decisions regardless of whether you understand these beliefs as fact, supernatural or theory. They shape your decisions if you hold them in your heart. Will they shape your decisions in order to attract the Blessings or the curses?

<u>Freedom of Choice</u>. **Choose that which is Good**

What you hold in your Heart starts in your Mind.

It is easy to make a decision to choose what is right. The mind receives information (experiences), processes the information (thinking), then you make a decision (choice). Always choose joy and choose what is the right thing to do.

As discussed in Chapter One: Choose the Joy of the Lord, not one of the two modes of happenstance: happiness or unhappiness. Next two (2) choices are the Lord or Satan, synonymous with good or evil. Always choose the Lord and that which is good and do the right thing. And, always do the right thing no matter what! Everybody can be doing the wrong thing. You are required to do the right thing.

Repeating Cycles and Behaviors

When events are occurring rapidly choices can be made out of habit, that is, with only minimal thought.

You need to get control of your decision making process. Here is the trap of repeating cycles and behaviors. You need to focus on events and become aware of habit decisions you are making during events that reoccur.

If, for example you discover that you just made a bad decision: you complained. Be prepared for the next time that type of event occurs to change your response: instead of complaining be prepared to give thanks and to praise the Lord and break the cycle. Then you begin to hold the Joy in your heart and begin to attract the Lord's Blessings.

Now moving on wholeheartedly into the next two (2) choices of choosing the Lord or choosing Satan, the same as good or evil. This is powerful! When you accept or reject the Lord, always remember that rejecting the Lord or the Lord's way is equivalent to choosing Satan and evil and to continue in sin:

The Word of the Lord <u>Convicts</u>: Two (2) Choices:

There absolutely is the Higher Power the Creator God, the Good Heavenly Father, the Holy One, the Redeemer, that actually truly exits! To grasp this precept of "what you hold in your heart then that is what you attract" you must understand that the Word of the Lord "convicts" a person and then you make one of the two choices: either to accept or reject the Lord:

The first choice is to accept the Lord and confess your sin and the Lord will redeem you. Absolutely! His jurisdiction is the heart and He desires that everyone to be saved.

When Apostle Peter preached after Pentecost they were "pricked in their heart" and then they repented:

▶ 36. Therefore let all the house of Israel know assuredly, that God hath made the same Jesus, whom ye have crucified, both Lord and Christ.

37. Now when they heard this, they were pricked in their heart, and said unto Peter and to the rest of the apostles, Men and brethren, what shall we do?

38. Then Peter said unto them, Repent, and be baptized every one of you in the name of Jesus Christ for the remission of sins, and ye shall receive the gift of the Holy Ghost.

39. For the promise is unto you, and to your children, and to all that are afar off, even as many as the Lord our God shall call.

40. And with many other words did he testify and exhort, saying, save yourselves from this untoward generation.

41. Then they that gladly received his word were baptized: and the same day there were added unto them about three thousand souls.

Acts 2: 36-41

CHAPTER 2

WHAT YOU HOLD IN YOUR HEART IS WHAT YOU ATTRACT

Again you have one of two choices when the word of the Lord "Convicts" a person. This second choice occurred after Apostle Stephen preached and they were "cut to the heart" they chose the second choice: to reject the Lord and continue in their sin:

▶ 54 When they heard these things, they were cut to the heart, and they gnashed on him with their teeth.

55. But he, being full of the Holy Ghost, looked up steadfastly into heaven, and saw the glory of God, and Jesus standing on the right hand of God,

56. and said, Behold, I see the heavens opened, and the Son of man standing on the right hand of God.

57. Then they cried out with a loud voice, and stopped their ears, and ran upon him with one accord,

58. and cast him out of the city, and stoned him....

Acts 7: 54-58

Choose the Lord. Choose the Lord's way. God gave you the ability to make decisions. Always choose to do the right thing, no matter what everyone else is doing! Choose the right way! You always do the right thing! Run from evil! Commit yourself to the Lord's ways.

Choose as those who listened to Apostle Peter preach the Gospel after Pentecost, who were "pricked in their heart" they repented. Choose to learn these precepts that are found in the Bible and enter into the Blessings, the Joy and the Protection of the Lord, the Good Heavenly Father, the Holy One who is the Higher Spirit who is the Creator of the Universe, the Redeemer.

Be Encouraged:

Be encouraged. Folks who are experiencing this for the first time, realizing that the Lord is truly powerful, able and is God Almighty be encouraged because this is not a hard thing. The same Lord loves us. He is also the Good Heavenly Father desiring for us to enter into His Joy and receive His Blessings. He is a Personal God who is always here for us. Also He is the Redeemer. He personally paid for our sins with His life. Along with His knowledge the Lord promises:

CHAPTER 2
WHAT YOU HOLD IN YOUR HEART IS WHAT YOU ATTRACT

▶ The fear of the Lord is the beginning of knowledge: but fools despise wisdom and instruction.

Proverbs 1:7

▶ For my yoke is easy, and my burden is light.

Matthew 11:30

▶ And he said, The things which are impossible with men are possible with God.

Luke 18:27

▶ And Jesus looking upon them saith, with men it is impossible, but not with God: for with God all things are possible.

Mark 10:27

What you hold in your heart then that is what you attract. The Lord will provide you the desires of your heart. The Creator God of the Universe, the Higher Power, the Holy One, the Redeemer that gives the power to choose. It starts in one's mind then moves to the heart.

Apostle Paul instructs us to think of good things.

▶ Finally, brethren, whatsoever things are true, whatsoever things are honest, whatsoever things are just, whatsoever things are pure, whatsoever things are lovely, whatsoever things are of good report; if there be any virtue, and if there be any praise, think on these things.

Philippians 4:8

Now you need to reflect on what you hold in your heart. Get right with the Lord. Repent of your sins to Jesus. He will forgive you. Desire the good things. Make an effort to hold the good things in your heart. The Lord helps you overcome.

WARNING: This is private. You do not share what you hold in your heart with others. As Jesus has warned us in the Gospel of Matthew:

Note: Rend means to separate or tear into parts.

▶ Give not that which is holy unto the dogs, neither cast ye your pearls before swine, lest they trample them under their feet, and turn again and rend you.

Matthew 7:6

CHAPTER 2
WHAT YOU HOLD IN YOUR HEART IS WHAT YOU ATTRACT

Not everyone will have encouraging words for the new believer. There are ones who will "rend" the new believer.

So what you desire in your heart is what the Creator God of the Universe, the Higher Power will give you or better put is that: He allows you to choose. Choose the Lord's way. Or, if you choose to permit your desire to be evil then what do you think you are going to get? Answer: Not the blessings. No way! You will receive evil! Then in continuing to desire evil where can that lead?

Answer: Reprobate

As Paul explains in his letter to the Romans "God gave them over to a reprobate mind"
Note: "**reprobate**" means wicked and worthless.

Note: Convenient means "proper."

▶ And even as they did not like to retain God in their knowledge, God gave them over to a reprobate mind, to do those things which are not convenient;

Romans 1:28

Reprobate does not include an apologetic heart that is remorseful and feels sorrowful over sin, as we are all sinners and fall short: Even ashamed to the Lord. The desire of the repentant heart was good not evil.

Whereas, a reprobate heart does "not like to retain God in their knowledge."

They were given over to a "reprobate mind" that is a wicked and worthless mind! It is dreadful to think of a person in such a lost state! Abandoned by God!

The Lord allows choice. So what you desire in your heart is what is attracted. If you choose to permit your desire to be evil then you do not the receive blessings. You receive evil! Apostle Paul explains in a letter to Titus:

Apostle Paul began/originated the Church in Crete. He could not stay there at the Church so he established Titus to lead the church congregation in Crete. Afterwards Paul sent a letter to instruct and encourage Titus.

In the letter Paul warns that some folks have knowledge of the Lord and His commandments but their works and their lives evidence minds that deny God. Because what they do is offensive, disobedient, and wicked.

CHAPTER 2
WHAT YOU HOLD IN YOUR HEART IS WHAT YOU ATTRACT

Apparently they love and desire their sins more than the Lord's way because they display no passion, no delight, no enthusiasm and no desire for the Lord or the Lord's way: Note: "reprobate" means wicked and worthless

▶ 15. Unto the pure all things are pure: but unto them that are defiled and unbelieving is nothing pure; but even their mind and conscience is defiled.

16. They profess that they know God; but in works they deny him, being abominable, and disobedient, and unto every good work reprobate.
Titus 1: 15-16

You have one of two choices when the word of the Lord "Convicts" a person. Denying the Lord and choosing to continue in sin brings about reprobate (wicked/worthless).

After Apostle Stephen preached and they were "cut to the heart" they chose to reject the Lord and continue in their sin whereas when Peter preached after Pentecost about three thousand souls gladly received His word and were baptized.

So maybe you have some work to do here. You are not alone. This is the work for all of us Christians. We need to focus and hold in our hearts good things.

Again be encouraged because it is the power of the Lord the Higher Power the Creator God, the Good Heavenly Father, the Holy One, the Redeemer that overcomes on our behalf! As Apostle John writes in a letter:

Note: "he that is in you" is the Lord.

Note: "he that is in the world" is Satan.

▶ Ye are of God, little children, and have overcome them: because greater is he that is in you, than he that is in the world.

1 John 4:4

He overcomes on our behalf and provides for us. Great is our reward and blessings here on earth as well as our reward and blessings to come in heaven as it is the will of Lord, the Good Heavenly Father, the Creator God of the Universe, the Higher Power, the Redeemer to give us such superior good things that are far better than what we could ever give one another, better than what we could ever obtain.

CHAPTER 2
WHAT YOU HOLD IN YOUR HEART IS WHAT YOU ATTRACT

We need to conform our desires to acceptable desires of the Lord, the Higher Power the Creator God, the Good Heavenly Father, the Holy One, the Redeemer, so that He can release the blessings described in Deuteronomy 28: 1-14.
The Lord's Blessings, the Lord's promise is for those that follow the Lord's commandments that His blessings shall come on thee, and "overtake thee" Deuteronomy 28: 2.

Be aware that we can limit, reduce or decrease our blessings! The Lord gives you the same measure of blessings, which you mete out (measure out) in giving to others!

A Giving Heart

Another example of the principles of what you hold in your heart is what you attract is in a "giving heart." The Lord provides you with the same measure of blessings that you mete out (measure out) in giving to others!

▶ Give, and it shall be given unto you; good measure, pressed down, and shaken together, and running over, shall men give into your bosom. For with the same measure that ye mete withal it shall be measured to you again.

Luke 6:38

Note: Take caution. Being taken advantage of is not giving. It is being beguiled, swindled and cheated.

The Blessings are from the Lord not from man. Abraham trusted in the Lord and refused the king of Sodom's offer of the spoils of victory. Abraham relied on the promise and covenant of God.

Note: shoelatchet is an old word for shoelace.

▶ That I will not take from a thread even to a shoelatchet, and that I will not take any thing that is thine, lest thou shouldest say, I have made Abram rich:

Genesis 14:23

Had Abraham taken the King's gift then after that it would not have been clear whether the Lord caused Abraham to prosper or whether it was the gift from the king of Sodom.

Think through giving and taking gifts, as it is a lot more involved than mostly one is aware.

Money: We should not just desire money in itself. But desire in our hearts the good things then the Lord provides away to get the good things to us and so money is just one of the many ways for the Lord to fulfill the desires of the good things held in our heart.

Holding in one's heart is what one attracts. When one seeks heavenly treasures one Tunes in Heaven and as a result attracts blessings and treasures:

▶ 19. Lay not up for yourselves treasures upon earth, where moth and rust doth corrupt, and where thieves break through and steal:

20. But lay up for yourselves treasures in heaven, where neither moth nor rust doth corrupt, and where thieves do not break through nor steal:

21. For where your treasure is, there will your heart be also.

Matthew 6:19-21

▶ For the love of money is the root of all evil: which while some coveted after, they have erred from the faith, and pierced themselves through with many sorrows.

1 Timothy: 6-10

King David's psalm, Psalm 37, praises these precepts to trust, delight and commit one's way to the way of the Lord and assures receiving the desires of one's heart:

▶ 3. Trust in the Lord, and do good; so shalt thou dwell in the land, and verily thou shalt be fed.

4. Delight thyself also in the Lord: and he shall give thee the desires of thine heart.

Psalm 37: 3-4

Blessings, Protection & Curses Extends to Those Nearby:

Blessings, Protections & Curses extends to those nearby. The Good Blessings that one attracts, flows and benefits those nearby. And, in addition there is protection: anyone cheating or offending the one whom the Lord is blessing experiences difficulty, stress and deficiency.

This was the case with Jacob. Those near to Jacob were benefited. And those cheating and offending Jacob were negatively affected, specifically Laban.

In Genesis, Laban was the father-in-law of Jacob, as he was the father of Rachel and Leah who were the wives of Jacob. Jacob is the one who was later re-named Israel.

WHAT YOU HOLD IN YOUR HEART IS WHAT YOU ATTRACT.

When Laban's sons accused Jacob of taking away all that was their father, Laban's. Jacob explained that his portion was "Blessed" for that reason the increase.

Jacob called Rachel and Leah to the field where he kept his flock. Jacob clarified to them that Laban, their father had cheated him out of wages over and over again. That he, Jacob had a dream and in the dream Jacob asked Laban to clarify his wages by either choosing speckled animals or ringstraked (streaked) animals as his wages. Then clearly the Lord blessed Jacob's portion with increase.

The account in Genesis of Jacob explaining to Rachel and Leah:

▶ 6. And ye know that with all my power I have served your father.

7. And your father hath deceived me, and changed my wages ten times; but God suffered him not to hurt me.

8. If he said thus, The speckled shall be thy wages; then all the cattle bare speckled: and if he said thus, The ringstraked shall be thy hire; then bare all the cattle ringstraked.

9. Thus God hath taken away the cattle of your father, and given them to me.

Genesis 31: 6-9

The Will of the Lord to give Blessings to Jacob could not be thwarted! Jacob received his Blessings!

Apostle Paul warns us to separate away from those who are disorderly, not walking in the way of the Lord:

▶ Now we command you, brethren, in the name of our Lord Jesus Christ, that ye withdraw yourselves from every brother who walketh disorderly and not according to the tradition which he received from us.

2 Thessalonians 3:6

He gives you the power to choose beliefs regardless of whether the beliefs are understood as fact, supernatural or theory. Choose beliefs that are consistent with the Word of the Lord. These beliefs then shape our decisions to choose which desires to hold in our heart and then there are the follow-on blessings or consequences

CHAPTER 3

~

EVIL THWARTED
JUSTICE/GOOD ACHIEVED

When evil is intended against you, then the Higher Power, the God of the universe, the Creator God, the Holy One, the Good Heavenly Father, the Redeemer that loves you, He thwarts the evil and brings about justice and makes good be achieved. He is our Protector, the Mighty One.

When evil is intended against you He redirects it back to sender and utterly destroys the evil or the Lord means it for good and brings it to pass to save you and many more people. He is our Protector, the Mighty One, He lets you enter into His Joy and gives you the desires of your heart and is wholly worthy. Tune-In Heaven. The Lord answers prayer!

The Higher Power, God Almighty, the Creator God, the Holy One, the Good Heavenly Father, the Redeemer, the Lord has the power to effect that which He please and it shall prosper where it is sent. As in Isaiah:

▶ 10. For as the rain cometh down, and the snow from heaven, and returneth not thither, but watereth the earth, and maketh it bring forth and bud, that it may give seed to the sower, and bread to the eater:

11. So shall my word be that goeth forth out of my mouth: it shall not return unto me void, but it shall accomplish that which I please, and it shall prosper in the thing whereto I sent it.

Isaiah 55:10-11

When evil is intended against you The Higher Power, The Protector, God Almighty, the Creator God, the Holy One, the Redeemer, thwarts the evil and brings about justice and makes good be achieved.

Haman:

In the Book of Esther the Lord redirects back to Haman the evil he intended against Mordecai. Haman hung on the very gallows he built to hang the good man, Mordecai and many lives were saved.

In ancient Persia, Haman one of the top officials calculated a plot to kill all of the Jews living in Persia and hang Mordecai a Jew on gallows. Mordecai was a good man. Haman built gallows fifty cubits high (about 85 feet high) to hang Mordecai. But the events turned against Haman.

Unbeknownst to Haman the King's wife, Queen Esther herself was a Jew and Haman's evil intentions were thwarted and redirected back to sender, and Haman was hanged from the very same gallows Haman built with the intentions to hang Mordecai. The Jews were saved. Then afterwards Haman's ten sons died in battle trying to kill the Jews. Their dead bodies were hanged on the very same gallows.

(Esther 7-Esther 9).

Joseph

When evil is intended against you The Higher Power, God Almighty, the Protector, the Creator God, the Holy One, the Good Heavenly Father, the Redeemer thwarts the evil and brings about justice and makes good be achieved.

In the Book of Genesis the Lord redirects the evil that was intended against Joseph by his brothers and all Israel was saved.

Jacob, who was renamed Israel, the founding father of ancient Israel, had twelve sons. Joseph was one of the sons. Ten of the other sons were very jealous of Joseph.

The father, Jacob loved Joseph more than his other sons. The father, Jacob gave Joseph a beautiful coat of many colors. Joseph had symbolic dreams that his brothers bowed to him. Even the Sun, Moon and stars bowed to Joseph in his dreams, which symbolically translates that his family was bowing to him. He told his brothers these dreams and it fueled the fire of jealousy!

Then one day Joseph met up with his brothers out in the fields tending the sheep. His brothers confronted him, pulled off of him his coat of many colors, cast him into a pit then sold him as a slave to merchants that were traveling by these ten sons of Israel.

The merchants sold Joseph as a slave in Egypt. He performed good work for his master, Potiphar. But Joseph was falsely accused of a crime and was put into a prison.

But events turn in Joseph's favor when brought up from prison to be in front of Pharaoh to interpret a dream.

Joseph interpreted Pharaoh's dream: "there will be seven years of bounty followed by seven years of famine."

Pharaoh was so impressed with Joseph's dream interpretation that he appointed Joseph to a position in the government of Egypt putting him in charge of storing food for the upcoming hard times.

Then after the seven years of bounty pass the famine came about. The brothers of Joseph showed up in Egypt looking for food. Joseph recognized his brothers. But his brothers did not recognize Joseph as their brother. They only saw Joseph as Pharaoh's powerful authority. When Joseph reveals himself to his brothers it is very compelling and heartfelt.

Then they were afraid because of Joseph's powerful position in Egypt. They were afraid of vengeance on them for what they had done to Joseph that is throwing Joseph into a pit then selling him as a slave.

CHAPTER 3
EVIL THWARTED - JUSTICE/GOOD ACHIEVED

However, Joseph has forgiveness in his heart and causes the bounty of Egypt to be shared with his family and all Israel was saved. Joseph revealed to his brothers that what they "meant for evil that the Lord meant for good":

But as for you, ye thought evil against me; but God meant it unto good, to bring to pass, as it is this day, to save much people alive.

Joseph

Joseph's brothers were in fear when they learned that they were in front of their brother Joseph the highest officer in Egypt, the one whom they sold into slavery.

▶ But as for you, ye thought evil against me; but God meant it unto good, to bring to pass, as it is this day, to save much people alive.

Genesis 50:20

Conviction.

When evil was intended against Joseph and Mordecai the Lord thwarted the evil and brought about justice and good was achieved.

Joseph's brothers in Egypt expressed their remorse and repented over their previous evil intensions against their own brother Joseph. They were "convicted" in their hearts. They were very sorry for what they had done to Joseph, similarly as to those that were convicted when Apostle Peter preached. Then all of Joseph's brothers, their families and their father, Isaiah moved into Egypt and were treated special by the Pharaoh. All of Israel was saved from the famine and prospered!

Whereas, neither Haman nor any of his ten (10) sons are accounted for as repented. In The Book of Esther, in the Old Testament of the Bible it is abundantly clear that Haman was made fully aware of the good deeds of Mordecai, such as Mordecai uncovering a plot to assassinate the king, and the king was saved. At one point Haman led the king's own horse, with Mordecai sitting on the horse through the city square, shouting, "This is what the king does for someone he wishes to honor!"

CHAPTER 3
EVIL THWARTED
JUSTICE/GOOD ACHIEVED

But nowhere in The Book of Esther was Haman or any of his sons accounted for as remorseful. Just like when Apostle Stephen preached those that were "convicted" gnashed their teeth, and continued in their sin. Haman was hanged on the gallows he had built to hang Mordecai.

And, Haman's ten (10) sons after they were killed then their bodies were hanged on those same gallows.

The Lord is our Protector, the Higher Power, the Mighty One, the Good Heavenly Father, the Redeemer. He redirects evil back to sender then utterly destroys the evil or He means it for good and brings it to pass to save you and many more people. He is our Protector, the Mighty One, He lets you enter into His Joy and gives you the desires of your heart and is wholly worthy. The Lord answers prayer!

Be aware when choices are presented, process the information and make a decision to obey the Lord's Commandments and Tune-In Heaven. Develop a personal relationship with the Higher Power, the Protector, God Almighty, the Good Heavenly Father, the Holy One, the Creator God, the Redeemer and enter into His Joy!

God Almighty, the Higher Power the Creator God, the Holy One, the Redeemer, the Lord is this power to effect that which He pleases and it shall prosper where it is sent.

The Lord's promise of protection as found in Isaiah:

▶ No weapon that is formed against thee shall prosper; and every tongue that shall rise against thee in judgment thou shalt condemn. This is the heritage of the servants of the Lord, and their righteousness is of me, saith the Lord.

Isaiah 54:17

The Lord's promise of protection in a song of King David:

▶ 14. The wicked have drawn out the sword, and have bent their bow, to cast down the poor and needy, and to slay such as be of upright conversation.

15. Their sword shall enter into their own heart, and their bows shall be broken.

Psalm 37: 14-15

The Higher Power, God Almighty, the Protector, the Good Heavenly Father, the Holy One, the Redeemer has the power to thwart evil and achieve good. No where else is the evidence so clear of evil being thwarted and justice and good achieved than when Jesus Christ of Nazareth, the Higher Power, the Creator God, the Holy One, the God Almighty, the Redeemer - walked on this earth.

When Jesus Christ of Nazareth, the Higher Power, the Creator God, the Holy One, God Almighty, the Redeemer - walked on this earth.

Jesus taught that from good comes good and from evil comes evil.

▶ 33. Either make the tree good, and his fruit good; or else make the tree corrupt, and his fruit corrupt: for the tree is known by his fruit.

34. O generation of vipers, how can ye, being evil, speak good things? for out of the abundance of the heart the mouth speaketh.

35. A good man out of the good treasure of the heart bringeth forth good things: and an evil man out of the evil treasure bringeth forth evil things.

Matthew 12: 33-35

Multitudes recognized Jesus as the Higher Power, the God Almighty, the Protector, the Creator God, the Holy One, the Redeemer when he walked on this earth. But others missed it or purposefully denied Him:

CHAPTER 3
EVIL THWARTED
JUSTICE/GOOD ACHIEVED

The scribes and Pharisees challenged the authenticity of Jesus and asked Him for proof by asking Him to show them a sign.

Now picture this: right in front of the eyes of the scribes and Pharisees, they are seeing Jesus Christ, the Higher Power, the Creator God, the Holy One, God Almighty, the Redeemer standing in front of them in plain view. Could they really just have not recognized Him?

Meanwhile, also in front of the Pharisees were the multitudes that had absolutely recognized Him and would testify as such.

"Throng" of people
Everywhere Jesus went there was a "throng" of people pressing in on Him from every side. A throng of people means a huge multitude of people. And, everywhere Jesus went He performed miracles, healing the sick, casting out demons and performed wonders like feeding multitudes and walking on the water. They all had witnessed His miracles.

Jesus "healed them all." All as in all! The Healings were not sporadic. Everyone was healed! As recorded in the Gospel of Mathew:

► ... and great multitudes followed him, and he healed them all;

Matthew 12:15

How many Healings, Demon's Expelled and things of Wonder were done by Jesus? Apostle John explains:

► And there are also many other things which Jesus did, the which, if they should be written every one, I suppose that even the world itself could not contain the books that should be written. Amen.

John 21: 25

In this context the scribes and Pharisees ask Jesus for proof by showing a sign. How could anyone miss it! Apparently these scribes and Pharisees must have intentionally not recognized Jesus.

CHAPTER 3
EVIL THWARTED
JUSTICE/GOOD ACHIEVED

Jesus knows the hearts of man. So when they asked Him to show a sign He replies as detailed in the Gospel of Matthew:
Note: the word generation also means other types of groupings of people as well, not just an age group.

▶ 38. Then certain of the scribes and of the Pharisees answered, saying, Master, we would see a sign from thee.

39. But he answered and said unto them, An evil and adulterous generation seeketh after a sign; and there shall no sign be given to it, but the sign of the prophet Jonas:

40. For as Jonas was three days and three nights in the whale's belly; so shall the Son of man be three days and three nights in the heart of the earth.

Matthew 12: 38-40

Comparing the Jonas experience to Jesus:

Jonas was swallowed by the whale. Then Jonas was spewed out after three (3) days. Jesus was crucified on the cross to death, buried in a tomb then Jesus rose on the third day. That was the promised sign. Wow!

How many Miracles and Wonders did Jesus perform?

The answer is the number of healings, casting out evil spirits and wonders were too many too document! The Apostle John reported about the multitude of the miracles and wonders that Jesus performed in the Gospel of John:

▶ And there are also many other things which Jesus did, the which, if they should be written every one, I suppose that even the world itself could not contain the books that should be written. Amen.

John 21:25

Jesus always had the Power to avoid the Cross: He Laid down His Life!

Evidenced on the first day of His Ministry Jesus miraculously avoids the loss of His Life:

Jesus announced the beginning of His ministry on the Sabbath Day in the synagogue in Nazareth, the city where Jesus had grown-up.

CHAPTER 3
EVIL THWARTED
JUSTICE/GOOD ACHIEVED

Jesus was rejected by those of the synagogue in Nazareth and they led him to the edge of a cliff to throw Him down. But Jesus miraculously just turns into the crowd, walks through the midst of the crowd and goes on His way!

▶ 28. And all they in the synagogue, when they heard these things, were filled with wrath,

29. And rose up, and thrust him out of the city, and led him unto the brow of the hill whereon their city was built, that they might cast him down headlong.

30. But he passing through the midst of them went his way,

Luke 4: 28-30

The first day of His Mission was clearly too soon to fulfill His scriptural sacrificial death. Jesus later on allowed Himself to be taken at the Garden of Gethsemane, then to the Cross.

At the Garden of Gethsemane, just prior to the Cross, the power of Jesus was evidenced when Jesus spoke "I am He" and Roman Soldiers were knocked down.

A number of men that came to take Jesus were knocked down to the ground by the voice of Jesus in the Garden of Gethsemane. Men out of the band of men and officers from the chief priests and Pharisees, men who had came with lanterns and torches and weapons to take Jesus, also along, present was Judas.

▶ As soon then as he (Jesus) had said unto them, I am he, they went backward, and fell to the ground.

John 18:6

He allowed Himself to be taken from the Garden of Gethsemane, be tried, sentenced and hung on the Cross.

On the cross Jesus laid down His life. He bowed His head and gave up the ghost as it is recorded in the Gospel of John:

▶… He said, It is finished: and he bowed his head, and gave up the ghost.

John 19:30

Apostle Paul testifies of 500 witnesses to the Resurrected Jesus:

The Apostle Paul was testifying to the Corinthians how that Jesus died for our sins according to the scriptures in a letter to the Corinthians that includes a list of witnesses to the Resurrected Jesus.

The list cites five hundred (500) at one time having witnessed the Resurrect Jesus:

Note: Cephas is another name for Apostle Peter.
Note: Fallen asleep of course means here that they died.

▶ 4. And that he was buried, and that he rose again the third day according to the scriptures:

5. And that he was seen of Cephas, then of the twelve:

CHAPTER 4

~

Come Into a Personal Relationship With the Higher Power The Holy One, the Redeemer

You can have a personal relationship with the Higher Power, the God of the Universe, the Creator God, the Holy One, the Redeemer. He is now reaching out to you as the prophet Isaiah declares: "God's arms are stretched out still." The stretched out arms of Jesus are now reaching out to you to enter into His Joy and receive His Blessings, Prosperity and Protection.

You can develop a personal relationship with God Almighty, the Higher Power, the Holy One, the Creator God, the Redeemer. Commit your way to the Lord and Obey the Lord's Commandments and Tune-In Heaven.

▶ And thou shalt love the Lord thy God with all thy heart, and with all thy soul, and with all thy mind, and with all thy strength: this is the first commandment. Mark 12:30

Remember to love the Lord is to keep His commandments:

▶ If ye love me, keep my commandments.

John 14:15

▶ And we know that all things work together for good to them that love God, to them who are the called according to his purpose.

Romans 8:28

In the Bible we can find instructions from those who trusted in the Lord, committed their way to the Lord and developed a personal relationship with the Higher Power, the Creator God, the Redeemer and they received His Joy, Blessings, Prosperity and Protection. Here are examples for us to follow:

King David's praises these precepts to trust, delight (no complaining) and commit one's way to the ways of the Lord, which assures receiving the desires of one's heart.

The Lord will bring upon righteousness. Evildoers will be cut off. Those that wait upon the Lord shall inherit the earth:

▶ 3. Trust in the Lord, and do good; so shalt thou dwell in the land, and verily thou shalt be fed.

4. Delight thyself also in the Lord: and he shall give thee the desires of thine heart.

5. Commit thy way unto the Lord; trust also in him; and he shall bring it to pass.

6. And he shall bring forth thy righteousness as the light, and thy judgment as the noonday.

7. Rest in the Lord, and wait patiently for him: fret not thyself because of him who prospereth in his way, because of the man who bringeth wicked devices to pass.

8. Cease from anger, and forsake wrath: fret not thyself in any wise to do evil.

9. For evildoers shall be cut off: but those that wait upon the Lord, they shall inherit the earth.

Psalm 37:3-9

To have a personal relationship with the Lord, to know the Lord, the Apostle Paul provides insight into the mind of the Lord. Paul asks: Who could provide the Lord with advice or provide credit so that God would have to repay?

Paul's letter to the Romans illustrates the Lord's knowledge wisdom, judgments and mind are beyond our understanding:

▶ 33. O the depth of the riches both of the wisdom and knowledge of God! How unsearchable are his judgments, and his ways past finding out!

34. For who hath known the mind of the Lord? or who hath been his counsellor?

35. Or who hath first given to him, and it shall be recompensed unto him again?

36. For of him, and through him, and to him, are all things: to whom be glory for ever. Amen.

Romans 11:33-36

CHAPTER 4
PERSONAL RELATIONSHIP
WITH THE HIGHER POWER

Also, No Complaining: Apostle Paul warns against complaining as he compares people as pots and the Lord as the potter who makes different pots on the potter's wheel:

▶ 20. ... Shall the thing formed say to him that formed it, Why hast thou made me thus?

21.Hath not the potter power over the clay, of the same lump to make one vessel unto honour, and another unto dishonour?

22. What if God, willing to shew his wrath, and to make his power known, endured with much longsuffering the vessels of wrath fitted to destruction:

23. And that he might make known the riches of his glory on the vessels of mercy, which he had afore prepared unto glory

Romans 9: 20-23

Also the Prophet Isaiah warns not to complain to the Lord about our purpose for which we were made in comparing people as pots and Lord as the pot maker:

▶9. Woe unto him that striveth with his Maker! Let the potsherd strive with the potsherds of the earth. Shall the clay say to him that fashioneth it, What makest thou? or thy work, He hath no hands?
Isaiah 45:9

To have a personal relationship with the Lord we desire to know the ways of the Lord.

Praise God! Thank you Jesus!

Sin.
So then We have this Problem called Sin.

▶ As it is written, There is none righteous, no, not one:
Romans 3:10

CHAPTER 4
PERSONAL RELATIONSHIP
WITH THE HIGHER POWER

Good thoughts attract that which is good: Blessings, the
Joy of the Lord, and plays the mainstream share in the
development of a personal relationship with the Higher
Power, the Creator God, the Redeemer and receiving His
Joy, Blessings, Prosperity and Protection.

To have a personal relationship with the Lord is to know
these precepts to trust, delight (no complaining) and
commit one's way to the ways of the Lord (following His
Commandments) or, otherwise, disobeying the Lord is
sin. Sin hinders us from knowing the Lord.

Jesus Fulfills the Law.
Jesus is not a Free Pass to Sin!

When Jesus came He Fulfilled the law. Jesus made it
known that the law would be here until the last days.
Many say in error that the law was nailed to the cross
with Christ. This is a lie from Satan. Do not believe such
a lie. It is not Biblical.

Jesus clearly explains that the law is going to be with us and we are required to obey the law, even required to obey the least of the Commandments. The Gospel of Matthew:

▶ 17. Think not that I am come to destroy the law, or the prophets: I am not come to destroy, but to fulfil.

18. For verily I say unto you, Till heaven and earth pass, one jot or one tittle shall in no wise pass from the law, till all be fulfilled.

19. Whosoever therefore shall break one of these least commandments, and shall teach men so, he shall be called the least in the kingdom of heaven: but whosoever shall do and teach them, the same shall be called great in the kingdom of heaven.

Matthew 5: 17-19

CHAPTER 4
PERSONAL RELATIONSHIP
WITH THE HIGHER POWER

Jesus explained the connection between anger and murder and the connection between lust and adultery.

Anger

Note: Raca means empty-headed, stupid – like an "air-head."

▶ 21.Ye have heard that it was said by them of old time, Thou shalt not kill; and whosoever shall kill shall be in danger of the judgment:

22. But I say unto you, That whosoever is angry with his brother without a cause shall be in danger of the judgment: and whosoever shall say to his brother, Raca, shall be in danger of the council: but whosoever shall say, Thou fool, shall be in danger of hell fire.

Matthew 5: 21-22

Lust

▶ 27. Ye have heard that it was said by them of old time, Thou shalt not commit adultery:

28. But I say unto you, That whosoever looketh on a woman to lust after her hath committed adultery with her already in his heart.

Matthew 5:27-28

It starts in your mind. You feel convicted. You make a choice. It travels to your heart. What you hold in your heart is what you attract. If you choose evil - you attract evil.

If you get angry most likely you will not commit murder. But anger attracts evil generally. Anger does not attract blessings it repels blessings. Similarly, lusting with one's eyes does not necessarily mean that adultery will follow. But blessings are repelled. Evil attracts evil generally. You get more evil.

Anger and lust are sins. Complaining is a sin as well. When one complains one is finding faults with one's own gifts.

CHAPTER 4
PERSONAL RELATIONSHIP
WITH THE HIGHER POWER

When one is not satisfied with one's gifts the next step is to look at the gifts of others. Complaining may not necessarily lead to jealously or coveting the gifts of others. But blessings are repelled. Jesus taught that evil begets evil. Evil attracts more evil and blessings are repelled.

Good thoughts are first in the process to attract His Joy, Blessings, Prosperity and Protection. And, plays the mainstream share in the development of a personal relationship with the Higher Power, the Creator God, the Redeemer.

Trust in the Lord and commit your ways to the Lord and follow His law. Otherwise, disobeying the Lord is sin. Sin hinders us from knowing the Lord and attracts evil.

The Lord Does Not Give Up On Us.

The Lord has given us the ability to make decisions. He has given us free choice. We choose to never give up on ourselves and commit our ways to the Lord, and then re-commit our ways to the Lord.

We sin and are remorseful, repentant and ashamed to the Lord. We are contrite and come to the Lord and He forgives our sin, as He knows our heart. We repeat, we repeat until we get it right. Eventually we overcome! Praise the Lord!

Find delight in following the Lord's commandments and love and thank the Lord for dying on the cross for our sins.

Control sin in your mind, before it reaches the heart, and before acting out sin. The Lord gave us the ability to choose. Choose what is right. And always do the right thing. Find delight in the ways of the Lord.

In Genesis the Lord explains to Cane to control his sin.

The Lord accepted Abel's offering. But the Lord did not accept Cane's offering. The Lord instructed Cane that Cane knew what to do, and that he needed to do what is well. Then the Lord warns Cane that sin is at the door. That Cane needed to master the sin or the sin would rule over him. Also take note that Cain is complaining:

Note: countenance means face, or facial expression.

▶ 5. But unto Cain and to his offering he had not respect. And Cain was very wroth, and his countenance fell.

6. And the LORD said unto Cain, Why art thou wroth? and why is thy countenance fallen?

7. If thou doest well, shalt thou not be accepted? and if thou doest not well, sin lieth at the door. And unto thee shall be his desire, and thou shalt rule over him.

Genesis 4: 5-7

So then if the sin rules over one then that person becomes a servant of sin.

▶ Jesus answered them, Verily, verily, I say unto you, Whosoever committeth sin is the servant of sin.

John 8:34

Jesus Came to "Preach Deliverance to the Captives:"

The Gospel of Luke reports that Jesus was anointed concerning a variety of matters including to "Preach Deliverance to the Captives:

▶ The Spirit of the Lord is upon me, because he hath anointed me to preach the gospel to the poor; he hath sent me to heal the brokenhearted, to preach deliverance to the captives, and recovering of sight to the blind, to set at liberty them that are bruised.

Luke 4:18

Who are the "captives" that Jesus talks about?

Answer: Sinners. Sinners are captive to sin, servants of sin, ruled over by the evil one. Jesus came to set the sinner free.

The Struggle of Apostle Paul with Sin:

Apostle Paul writes of his own personal struggle with sin and his answer to call upon the name of the Lord to be saved in his letter the Romans.

By the way, it is encouraging for many Christians that even the Apostle Paul, the relentless advocate of Jesus Christ, struggled with sin just like the rest of us.

His struggle is truly heart-felt, as he sincerely desired to do what was right but apparently fell short.

Apostle Paul gave the answer, which in our hearts we all know: "to call upon the name of the Lord."

Apostle Paul's description of his own personal struggle with sin in his letter the Romans.

▶ 19. For the good that I would I do not: but the evil which I would not, that I do.

20. Now if I do that I would not, it is no more I that do it, but sin that dwelleth in me.

21. I find then a law, that, when I would do good, evil is present with me.

22. For I delight in the law of God after the inward man:

23. But I see another law in my members, warring against the law of my mind, and bringing me into captivity to the law of sin, which is in my members.

24. O wretched man that I am! Who shall deliver me from the body of this death?

Romans 7:19-24

▶ For whosoever shall call upon the name of the Lord shall be saved.
Romans 10:13

CHAPTER 4
PERSONAL RELATIONSHIP
WITH THE HIGHER POWER

Apostle Paul warns to stay free of sin:

▶ Stand fast therefore in the liberty wherewith Christ hath made us free, and be not entangled again with the yoke of bondage.

Galatians 5:1

Be encouraged:

Be encouraged. For folks who are experiencing this for the first time, realizing that the Lord is truly powerful, able and is God Almighty. This is not a hard thing. The same Lord loves us. He is also the Good Heavenly Father desiring for us to enter into His Joy and receive His Blessings. He is a Personal God who is always here for us. Also He is the Redeemer.

He personally paid for our sins with His life.

Along with the Lord's knowledge and His promises, He encourages:

▶ And he said, The things which are impossible with men are possible with God.

Luke 18:27

▶ For my yoke is easy, and my burden is light.

Matthew 11:30

▶ The fear of the Lord is the beginning of knowledge: but fools despise wisdom and instruction.

Proverbs 1:7

▶ And Jesus looking upon them saith, with men it is impossible, but not with God: for with God all things are possible.

Mark 10:27

CHAPTER 4
PERSONAL RELATIONSHIP
WITH THE HIGHER POWER

Prelude\Forward to The Sinner's Prayer.

The guidance is to call upon the name of the Lord and to repent. There is no named "Sinner's Prayer" in the Bible. Though, the Sinner's Prayer is real. It includes the Biblical guidance to call upon the name of the Lord and repent. There are many variations of the Sinner's Prayer. The fundaments: You need to call upon the name of the Lord and to repent.

Are you committed to making positive changes in your life that impact and connect you to receiving the Blessings of the Good Heavenly Father, the Protection of God Almighty, and entering into the Joy of the Lord, the Higher Power, the Creator God, the Holy One, the Redeemer?

Following the Lord is not a burden but a joy! We delight in the Lord's precepts. We find joy in following

His commandments: The Lord instructs: "if you love me follow my commandments."

John 14:15

Control the sin in your heart before it takes control and becomes your master.

You have choice all the time: The God given ability to make decisions. Always choose what is right and do the right thing. You do the right thing no matter what everyone else is doing around you. You are always required to do the right thing.

One suffers the consequences of sinful actions. You desired it. You acted the evil out. You get the evil consequences: The curses, frustration, confusion, loss, sorrow, heartaches even death are the consequences of sin/evil actions. These consequences are real. Also the patterns and cycles repeat. You get stuck.

How does it stop?

Answer: Call upon the name of the Lord and repent!

We serve a just God. So we need to be redeemed by a Savior. The Lord suffered unto his death to redeem us. He took the punishment we deserve to make us acceptable to a just God.

Some say, "Shout it out!" You do not need to "Shout it out." That depends on you and your surroundings.
But of course it is ok to shout it out. It is up to you.

WARNING: This is private. You do not share what you hold in your heart with others. As Jesus has warned us in the Gospel of Matthew:
Note: Rend means to separate or tear into parts.

Not everyone will have encouraging words for the new believer. There are ones who will "rend" the new believer.

► Give not that which is holy unto the dogs, neither cast ye your pearls before swine, lest they trample them under their feet, and turn again and rend you.

Matthew 7:6

The Lord's jurisdiction is the heart. It is always between you and the Lord. First read through the Sinner's Prayer on the next page, which is the Sinner's Prayer that I recommend. Which I think is perfect. You decide. Make changes if you like.

You certainly can personalize the Sinner's Prayer as it is between you and the Lord. You just need the two fundaments: Calling upon the name of the Lord and repenting. Praise you Father, Son and Holy Spirit!

If you are ready: call upon the name of the Lord and repent.

The Sinner's Prayer

Dear Jesus, I call upon Your name Jesus, God Almighty, the Good Heavenly Father, the Higher Power the Creator God, the God of the Universe, the Holy One, the Holy Spirit, the Redeemer, the God of Abraham, Isaac and Jacob.

Thank you for convicting me of sin, in my mind, in my heart and in my actions. You loved me while I was still in sin.

I want to turn away from sin and commit my way to Your way, Lord and to trust in You, Lord. Please forgive me, I am genuinely sorry, I desire to do what is right from now on, help me avoid sinning again.

Good Heavenly Father, I need your help. Please save me from the bondage of sin, save me from the curses, frustration, confusion, loss, sorrow, heartaches, further consequences of sin/evil actions and end the repeating patterns and cycles.

I desire positive changes in my life, to receive the Blessings, and the Prosperity of the Good Heavenly Father, and the Protection of God Almighty, and the Joy of the Lord.

I believe that your son, Jesus Christ died for my sins, was resurrected from the dead, is alive, and hears my prayer. Please Jesus become the Lord of my life. Rule and reign in my heart from this day forward. Let Your Will be done through me. Holy Spirit come dwell in me to empower me to obey God's commandments.

In Jesus name I pray. Praise you Father, Son and Holy Spirit. Thank you Jesus!
Amen.